A Survival Manual
for Medical Students

As you begin your medical studies,
this book is presented with the best wishes of
WYETH LABORATORIES,
makers of pharmaceuticals, nutritionals,
antibiotics, and biologicals

Wyeth Laboratories
P.O. Box 8299
Philadelphia, Pennsylvania 19101

A Survival Manual for Medical Students

By the Committee on Medical Education,
Group for the Advancement of Psychiatry

Mental Health Materials Center
P.O. Box 304, Bronxville, N.Y. 10708

Library of Congress Cataloging in Publication Data
Main entry under title:

A Survival manual for medical students.

(Publication / Group for the Advancement of Psy-
chiatry ; v. 11, 2nd = no. 108)
    1. Medical colleges—Psychological aspects.   2. Medical
students—Psychology.   3. Success.   I. Group for the
Advancement of Psychiatry. Committee on Medical Education.
II: Series: Publication (Group for the Advancement of
Psychiatry) ; no. 108.
R737.S86   610'.7'39   82-6406
ISBN 0-910958-12-2   AACR2

Volume XI, Publication No. 108

This is the second in a series of publications comprising Volume XI.

For information on availability of this publication, please contact the Mental
Health Materials Center, 30 East 29th Street, New York, NY 10016.

Manufactured in the United States of America

Illustrations by Doug Anderson

Cover Art by Willi Baum

FIRST EDITION
        First printing: July 1982
        Second printing: July 1983
        Third printing: June 1984
        Fourth printing: June 1985
        Fifth printing: June 1986
        Sixth printing: May 1987
        Seventh printing: May 1988
        Eighth printing: July 1990

Contents

Foreword

Being a physician is, at its best, intellectually challenging, emotionally rewarding, and socially esteemed. The development of a college graduate into a physician is one of the most exciting transformations a human being can experience. But sometimes it hurts. Regardless of their promise and the anticipation of the outcome, most medical students experience some pain, doubt, anxiety, or depression. The reasons vary from one person to another, and so do the coping strategies that get students through. But some common elements have been recognized in the problem, and analysis of them has led to the preparation of this book. I think every medical student will get something out of it. If you are among the majority of students who sooner or later experience these feelings, you will understand them better and find useful suggestions for responding to your bad days and increasing your good ones. And if you're in the small group of students who never have a bad day, you'll at least understand your classmates better and be able to help them—which is pretty good practice for being a physician.

Daniel D. Federman, M.D.
Dean for Students and Alumni,
Professor of Medicine,
Harvard Medical School
Boston, Massachusetts

Statement of Purpose

THE GROUP FOR THE ADVANCEMENT OF PSYCHIATRY has a membership of approximately 300 psychiatrists, most of whom are organized in the form of a number of working committees. These committees direct their efforts toward the study of various aspects of psychiatry and the application of this knowledge to the fields of mental health and human relations.

Collaboration with specialists in other disciplines has been and is one of GAP's working principles. Since the formation of GAP in 1946 its members have worked closely with such other specialists as anthropologists, biologists, economists, statisticians, educators, lawyers, nurses, psychologists, sociologists, social workers, and experts in mass communication, philosophy, and semantics. GAP envisages a continuing program of work according to the following aims:

1. To collect and appraise significant data in the fields of psychiatry, mental health, and human relations

2. To reevaluate old concepts and to develop and test new ones

3. To apply the knowledge thus obtained for the promotion of mental health and good human relations

GAP is an independent group, and its reports represent the composite findings and opinions of its members only, guided by its many consultants.

SURVIVAL MANUAL FOR MEDICAL STUDENTS was formulated by the Committee on Medical Education which acknowledges on page xii the participation of others in the preparation of this report. The members of this committee and the members of the other GAP committees, as well as additional membership categories and current and past officers of GAP, are listed below:

COMMITTEE ON MEDICAL EDUCATION

Paul Tyler Wilson, Bethesda, Md., Chairperson
David R. Hawkins, Chicago, Ill.*
Harold Lief, Philadelphia, Pa.
Carol Nadelson, Boston, Mass.
Herbert Pardes, Rockville, Md.
Carolyn Robinowitz, Bethesda, Md.
Jeanne Spurlock, Washington, D.C.
Bryce Templeton, Philadelphia, Pa.
Sidney L. Werkman, Denver, Colo.
Sherwyn M. Woods, Lost Angeles, Calif.

*Upon completion of this report Dr. Hawkins succeeded as Chairperson of this committee.

COMMITTEE ON ADOLESCENCE

Warren J. Gadpaille, Englewood, Colo., Chairperson
Ian A. Canino, New York, N.Y.
Harrison P. Eddy, New York, N.Y.
Sherman C. Feinstein, Highland Park, Ill.
*Maurice R. Friend, New York, N.Y.
Michael Kalogerakis, New York, N.Y.
Clarice J. Kestenbaum, New York, N.Y.
Derek Miller, Chicago, Ill.
Silvio J. Onesti, Belmont, Mass.

*Deceased

COMMITTEE ON AGING

Charles M. Gaitz, Houston, Tex., Chairperson
Gene D. Cohen, Rockville, Md.
Lawrence F. Greenleigh, Los Angeles, Calif.
George H. Pollock, Chicago, Ill.
Harvey L. Ruben, New Haven, Conn.
F. Conyers Thompson, Jr., Atlanta, Ga.
Jack Weinberg, Chicago, Ill.

COMMITTEE ON CHILD PSYCHIATRY

John F. McDermott, Jr., Honolulu, Hawaii, Chairperson
Paul L. Adams, Louisville, Ky.
James M. Bell, Canaan, N.Y.
Harlow Donald Dunton, New York, N.Y.
Joseph Fischhoff, Detroit, Mich.
Joseph M. Green, Madison, Wis.
Theodore Shapiro, New York, N.Y.

COMMITTEE ON THE COLLEGE STUDENT

Robert L. Arnstein, Hamden, Conn., Chairperson
Varda Backus, La Jolla, Calif.
Myron B. Liptzin, Chapel Hill, N.C.
Malkah Tolpin Notman, Brookline, Mass.
Gloria C. Onque, Pittsburgh, Pa.
Elizabeth Aub Reid, Cambridge, Mass.
Kent E. Robinson, Towson, Md.
Earle Silber, Chevy Chase, Md.

COMMITTEE ON CULTURAL PSYCHIATRY

Andrea K. Delgado, New York, N.Y., Chairperson
Ronald M. Wintrob, Farmington, Conn.

COMMITTEE ON THE FAMILY

Henry U. Grunebaum, Cambridge, Mass., Chairperson
W. Robert Beavers, Dallas, Tex.
Ellen M. Berman, Merion, Pa.
Ivan Boszormenyi-Nagy, Wyncote, Pa.
Lee Combrinck-Graham, Philadelphia, Pa.
Ira D. Glick, New York, N.Y.
Frederick Gottlieb, Los Angeles, Calif.
Charles A. Malone, Cleveland, Ohio
Joseph Satten, San Francisco, Calif.

COMMITTEE ON GOVERNMENTAL AGENCIES

Sidney S. Goldensohn, Jamaica, N.Y., Chairperson,
James P. Cattell, Monterey, Mass.
Naomi Heller, Washington, D.C.
Roger Peele, Washington, D.C.
William W. Van Stone, Palo Alto, Calif.

COMMITTEE ON HANDICAPS

Norman R. Bernstein, Chicago, Ill., Chairperson
Betty J. Pfefferbaum, Houston, Tex.
George Tarjan, Los Angeles, Calif.
Thomas G. Webster, Washington, D.C.
Henry H. Work, Washington, D.C.

Committee Acknowledgments

For their invaluable help in formulating this publication, the Committee would like to express their appreciation:

To Barbara Long, one of our GAP Fellows and currently resident at the Institute of Living, for her wisdom and energy in writing, editing, field-testing, and preparing drafts of this manual in its developmental period;

To Charles Seashore, Ph.D., consultant on experiential learning, for his inspiration and clarity about the importance of the balance between stress and nurturance for people in the throes of medical education;

And to Karen Hopenwasser, our other GAP Fellow, for her participation in the editorial process that led to the culmination of this work.

Paul Wilson, *Chairperson*
Committee on Medical Education

1

Introduction

Getting a degree in medicine takes four short years. We begin the process feeling just like everybody else in the world—squeamish at the sight of blood and vomitus or at the idea of hurting someone or at the prospect of peering at people's unclad bodies. We seek to end up four years later calm, knowledgeable, and effective physicians.

The transformation can happen so fast, primarily, because it happens so intensely. We encounter an overwhelming barrage of events from Day 1 of medical school until the end. The impact of these events is always the same: to remove the parts of us that get in the way of our being good doctors and to add whatever parts we lack. The process feels about as disruptive as it sounds.

The key to surviving in medical school, then, lies in letting the events change you without destroying you or even causing you too much pain. How? To answer that question, let us first consider six elements involved in stressful medical school events:

- the pre-set
- stress-events
- strain-reactions
- first aid
- back-up support and
- preventive maintenance.

1

The *pre-set* consists of early life programming that makes a training event particularly rough for *you*. We each have our own programming from childhood and adolescence. As a result, an event that is especially stressful for you may have no effect at all on your classmates, and vice versa. Some programming, though, is almost universal in our culture (e.g., "Thou shalt not stick thy finger into someone else's rectum"), and so you will sometimes find everyone in your class shuddering when you shudder.

A *stress-event* is any event that triggers a strain-reaction in *you*. It is rarely intrinsically stressful. That is, it almost never involves physical pain or deprivation or fatigue. Stress-events are stressful because you are programmed to experience them that way.

A *strain-reaction* is whatever your particular reaction happens to be to a stress-event. Again, individuality is the key word. To the same stress-event, for example, some medical students may react with anxiety, others may look calm but simmer inside, and a few may be free of any reaction at all.

First-aid is whatever you do to help yourself recover from a strain-reaction. Some first-aid strategies lead to rapid recovery, such as growth, confidence, and resiliency. Other strategies can make you fearful, cold, or tense. Needless to say, we will later describe which strategies do what.

Back-up support is all of the human warmth, direction, sympathy, demonstration, defending, kindly questioning, and love that carries you through medical school.

Preventive maintenance is whatever you do when you are *out* of the role of medical student (and later of physician) to keep yourself fulfilled, refreshed, enthusiastic, and effective when you are *in* it.

To return to the question, "How do you survive medical school?" You do it by learning gradually about your pre-set and how it has made you especially vulnerable to some stresses. You let yourself know when you are having a strain-reaction. You get first-aid fast when it happens. You make sure your relationships with the people who provide your back-up support are in good shape. And you make preventive maintenance an important part of your life style.

If this process goes well—and it will if you work at it—you will not only survive medical school, but you will also boost your odds for emerging from it an effective, comfortable physician well on the way toward continuing professional growth.

2

Pre-set

The pre-set consists of attitudes, expectations, and coping styles that have two prominent features: (1) They helped us (and/or our families) get along in the world and therefore we tend to view them as the "only way to be/think/feel." (2) They cause us to be at risk for psychological trouble whenever they are seriously breached, challenged, or overwhelmed. In short, they helped us during our earlier years but hinder us in medical school.

We all have our own individual pre-sets. That is because we have each lived our unique lives before entering medical school. The best way to cope with your particular pre-set is to know what it is. Then come to some kind of peace with it, if you can. In the process of accepting it, you can soften it, integrate it, and make it less interfering.

To start you on your own self-discovery process, we have listed a few themes common to most medical students. See if we have included yours.

My son/daughter the ( ) doctor

Your family, like all families—whether they know it or not—harbors fantasies about what your being in medical school means to them. If you graduate, you will do great things for them because of those fantasies. But if you fail, you do them grievous harm somehow for the same reason. To make matters even more complicated, their fantasies about your success might also contribute to your *failing* from time to time. For instance:

My son/daughter the (soon-to-be-wealthy) doctor. If you are from a wealthy family, this may or may not be a particularly stressful expectation. Failure in medical school means having to go to another kind of graduate school—law perhaps—or maybe settling for a partnership in the family firm. But if, like most medical students, you are from a not-so-wealthy family, the personal impact of failing in medical school (very rare) or fearing that you might fail (very common) can be even more devastating because of the lack of options.

Some families think their whole status in society will magically blossom if "somebody makes it" into medicine. Other families put themselves into debt in order to finance "their" medical student. This will get worse in the future instead of better as the federal government discontinues its previous underwriting of medical education. Some families pin their hopes for ultimate financial security on producing a physician. "To fail in medical school," goes the message, "is to doom those poor loved ones to a life of poverty." *Their* security suddenly becomes *your* responsibility.

My son/daughter the (traitorous) doctor. Most of the attitudes we list here put pressure on you to succeed. This one can pressure you to *fail*.

What kind of families want their children to fail in medical school? Almost none want it consciously. But for those families that view medicine as alien or overpowering, to see their offspring succeed in medical school is to see them slip away from the family. "Doctors are too smart (or rich or powerful or confident or authoritarian or just different) to be one of us." Some families who, because of their backgrounds and values, may be very uncomfortable with the social prestige and economic status they imagine doctors have. They may resent that you know things they don't know or that you have achieved more than they. They may fear that *you* will no longer want to be part of *them*.

If your family has some of those feelings, you may get confusing mixed signals from them: "Do well but not too well" is a recurring kind of message. You also may get strangely cool receptions when you visit home again. Not open hostility, usually, but subtle words and actions that deflate the pride you would otherwise feel in your accomplishments. You find you begin to feel oddly depressed about your growing abilities in medicine.

My son/daughter the (brilliant) doctor. "Brilliance" does not describe mere intelligence or insight or knowledge or wit. It somehow combines them all into a magical alloy of omnipotent worth. Whoever in your family harbors doubts about his or her own intelligence or insight (and who does not?) may endow you with this quality. "If I don't have it, at least my son/daughter has." Imagine the doubts they will feel about themselves if you get a mediocre grade or two . . . to say nothing of what will happen if you fail entirely.

Trying to maintain a reputation of brilliance for your family can push you to fail as well as to succeed in medical school. This can happen especially if you are trying to free yourself from valuing too much your family's approval or disapproval.

My son/daughter the (miraculously curative) doctor. This one usually exists, though subtly, in every family where someone has (or is afraid of having) illness in general or some special illness in particular, especially cancer and heart attacks. This probably includes your family, too, since such fears tend to be universal. Your failure in medical school, of course, is felt as bringing death to your loved ones.

Another form of this pre-set may be family expectations that you can be "miraculously curative" while still a medical student. For example, you may be assumed to have mastered vast amounts of medical knowledge—maybe even more than the family physician—to answer their backlog of unanswered medical questions and complaints. This can lead to terrible disappointment (theirs) and embarrassment (yours) when the awful truth emerges: You are not only not "miraculously curative" but not even a fully trained doctor.

My son/daughter the (chip off the old block) doctor. Being a doctor's son or daughter in medical school is a mixed blessing. The sense of tradition and extra parental understanding of your struggles can be a boost. What is hard are the underlying dangers of *feeling fraudulent* ("I probably wouldn't have gotten into medical school if Dad/Mom hadn't been a doctor."); *competition* ("Hey [son or daughter], you did almost as well in gross anatomy as I did!"); *pressure to succeed* ("I know it's rough: I've been through it. But if I could make it, so can you!"); and *pressure to follow parental career* ("Well, someone's got to do the dermatology, I suppose, but it sure is a far cry from my general surgery practice!"). Your doing *too* well in medical school can evoke some uncomfortable messages from your doctor-parent, too, if his or her medical school career was not as spectacular as yours.

My son/daughter the (traditionally-married) doctor. It has always been difficult to combine medical school with marriage. It is even tougher

now that family roles are not automatically determined by gender. There are many questions and problems... like... "Who is the professional in the family?" "Who is going to earn the bigger income?" "Whose job takes precedence when attractive out-of-town residencies are proffered?" "Why do family events have to be planned around hospital on-call schedules?" "When (if ever) is the time to have kids?" "Who will watch them when Mommy/Daddy is on duty?"

These are tough kinds of issues to confront if you, your spouse, or both of you have traditional views about marriage. It is especially tough if either or both sets of in-laws have and express them as well.

At the top

The pressure to perform—to be Number One—to be at the top—exists in many forms:

- "I've always been at the top because if feels good and I like it."
- "My family wants me to be at the top." (See also "My son/daughter the (   ) doctor.")
- "If I'm not at the top I feel bad/weak/unlovable/ugly/sinful/worthless."

- (a corollary of #3) "I am worthwhile only when I am at the top."

Most of us who enter medical school have some of all four.

You have probably spent much of your life at the top. Otherwise you would not have been accepted into medical school. Unfortunately, so have your classmates. This means that—unless you are among the lucky ones—you will feel uncomfortable at grading time. "Failure," "lazy," "undedicated," "stupid," are some of the names of the pangs you will feel. And knowing that you are in good company farther down the bell-shaped curve (i.e., with the rest of your class) does not always help much. It can feel humiliating.

Mastery

This is a corollary of "At the top." It is a personal expectation that "I can and must understand/accomplish everything assigned to me with absolute completeness." Believing this can cause serious problems, because, with a few rare and pleasant exceptions, there is no way you can possibly master completely the volume of material you will encounter during the next four years.

To work is to succeed

"You can accomplish anything you want if you will just work hard enough." That is a useful axiom that gives physicians an extra push from within when they need it. However, when it is overdone, it can also lead to workaholism, unrealistic expectations, and other self-defeating behavior. Such a drive for work collapses (and so do its victims) when the workers run out of hours in the day.

Withdrawal

Being too close to people can be a great burden. They cry, complain, nag, wheedle, demand, threaten, and arouse our sympathies and our desires to rescue them. By the time we get to medical school, though, all of us have adjusted by learning a thousand skillful ways to put psychological distance around ourselves.

In medical training—particularly in our direct contacts with patients—distance has both positive and negative aspects. It is useful

when patients ask for more than the 100 percent we have to give. But it can also get in the way. Especially when we really *must* open ourselves up to the feelings of our patients—either to examine and understand them well enough to make an accurate diagnosis or to encounter them with the tenderness (and sometimes the firmness) that adequate medical care requires.

Man/Woman

Many people feel that sex role stereotypes are declining, perhaps in part because of the Women's Movement and the Counterculture Revolution of the late 1960s. Men find they do not always have to be aggressive and fearless. They can be tender, sensitive, and tearful. Women do not have to be passive and helpless. They can be assertive, challenging, and decisive.

However, you may suddenly find your early programming in conflict with the social demands of the situation, whether at home or at

school. If you are a male student who recognizes that medicine is, at least in part, a nurturant profession, you may feel uncomfortable with this expression of a "feminine characteristic." Similarly, if you are a female student who succeeds in the "masculine" profession of medicine, you may feel that you have had to give up part of your femininity in order to be accepted by colleagues. In either case, you may discover resentment contaminating your feelings about a partner who does not view your being a medical student as an automatic reason for you to be excused from all household responsibilities.

Doctors are magical

This notion is based on numerous inaccurate fantasies about doctors and doctoring. We will just list a few of them because they are self-explanatory:

- Doctors know everything
- Doctors can do anything
- Doctors are always cool, calm, and collected

These parts of our pre-set usually do not cause trouble until we start to *feel* like doctors—usually some time during our third or fourth years of medical school. Then—when we discover how little these fantasies seem to apply to the doctor-we-have-become—we feel some

very disquieting doubts. "Either I'm doing it wrong," we say to ourselves, "or I've been told some big lies about doctors."

It is really not surprising that we harbor these crazy notions. Every doctor we have ever seen on television embodies them magnificently. Also, in well-concealed corners of our souls, we passionately wish those fantasies were true.

3

Stress-events

Here is a list of stress-events that happen to most of us sooner or later in medical school. It would be a mistake to think of them simply as threats or nuisances. More accurately, they are challenges which, having been weathered successfully, help us to grow into the role of doctor. Whether they help you grow or whether they grind you down depends on how well you make use of good first-aid and back-up support in coping with them.

Threat of failure

This may be the most encompassing stress-event. It is every-where, ever-present, ever-intimidating . . . when you think you have failed an exam, when the gross anatomy specimen to be identified resembles nothing you have ever seen before, when you draw a blank on the pathology slide.

It is universal stress because of several features of medical schools:

- There are not many objective ways to measure how well you are doing. "Good" and "bad" performance is often a subjective judgment . . . and the faculty makes the call.

- For better and for worse, medical schools are authoritarian institutions. And so if you perform poorly too often, or too spectacularly, or too non-compliantly, you become a *persona non grata*.
- Since medical school is difficult, you will usually harbor a feeling that you are doing badly—even when you are doing comparatively well.

The pre-set attitude most severely struck by this stress-event is "My son/daughter the (   ) doctor" (q.v.). To have survived the academic rigors of pre-med only to be expelled from medical school is unimaginable. "How could I do such a thing?" "What will my family think?"

Threat of success

Strangely titled for a "threat," this stress-event comes up most often in four kinds of situations:

- When success threatens to propel you from the fairly comfortable role of the learning/observing/non-responsible student into the frightening role of doing/worrying/definitely-responsible physician,
- When success confirms yet again that you are the embodiment of your family's high expectations . . . just when you were striving to become a free-standing individual,
- When you get the feeling that you can be successful only at the expense of causing others to be unsuccessful, and
- When you feel that being a success makes you a highly visible target.

Too much work

This is probably the number one collaborator with "threat of failure," and so it is a very important stress. The reason you *think* there is too much work is that there really *is*. On the other hand, considering that you are trying to become a doctor in the remarkably short span of four years, the work load is almost too light.

Your work overload will change during medical school. In the first two years there are too many exams, too many facts, too many labs,

and too much lecture material. In the last two years there are too many work-ups, too many patients, and too many menial tasks.

If "mastery" and "to work is to succeed" figure prominently in your personal pre-set (as it is with most medical students), this stress can throw you into any and all of the strain-reactions listed later. Get first-aid *fast* when it starts.

At the bottom

This stress, not surprisingly, strikes hardest at those of us who aspire to be "at the top." But being at the bottom has two separate and equally negative meanings in medical school:

- If you have a low academic standing in your class, it is easy to conclude you are not doing well. However, considering who gets into medical school these days, you may be doing well even when you are at the very bottom.
- When you get to the clinical years of school (usually the last two years), all medical students are at the bottom—even if they are at the very top of their class. Attending physicians, house officers, nurses, janitors—everyone outranks us.

Feeling different

The medical profession, like the priesthood, is set apart by society. It empowers us to do things that no one else may do: inflict pain, ignore others' modesty, prescribe powerful drugs, and ask personal questions. For that reason alone you start to feel (and are looked upon by others) as a little different as soon as you start medical school. Add to that the fact that you are studying harder than your non-medical friends, that medical training involves about eight years of transient living, and that many years still separate you from an at-least-normal income, and you can begin to feel really different.

Feeling different is uncomfortable enough if you are a male of the ethnic majority. Imagine how if feels if you are a woman, belong to an ethnic minority, speak with an accent, or have a physical impairment. For you, feeling different from your classmates as well as from the rest of society can be one of the greatest stresses you will encounter in medical school. This stress is accentuated if your "differentness" interferes with the way people react to you.

Cadaver

By the time you read this booklet, you probably will already have met your cadaver, given him/her a name, and learned to your dismay that he/she was not constructed strictly according to *Gray's Anatomy*. You will also have learned that working with cadavers does not usually involve a lot of ongoing stress (though everyone secretly wonders how that first gross anatomy lab is going to go). But it is a rite of passage. Classmates and faculty may not think so (they've all been through it), but the rest of the world knows. We are virtually the only group empowered by our culture to learn directly from the dead the secrets of our construction.

Basic scientists

We are all unique. Such individuality expands and enriches our existence, as we meet others with whom we share common interests. Yet sometimes we meet people who seem like aliens. For example, during the first two years of medical school, you will meet many basic

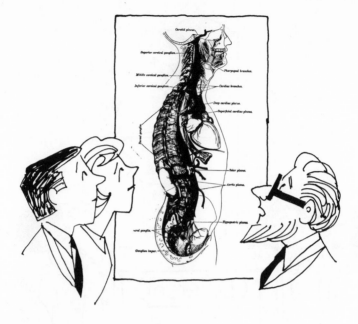

scientists. Some of them may have values that seem strange to you. In lectures, for example, some may enthusiastically describe microanatomical and biochemical subtleties that do not seem to you to have much to do with the practice of medicine. They will invite you to join them in their enthusiasm by having you do esoteric things in their labs and by memorizing whole sequences of things that are hard to understand and harder still to pronounce.

This may stir up some tensions within you. The ideal clinician— warm, efficient, and undistracted by scientific musings irrelevant to his vital mission—does not feel comfortable with the scientist's objectivity, meandering curiosity, and ceaseless cycles of discovery, classification, re-classification, and new discovery.

There is no simple remedy for these tensions. It may help, though, to keep reminding yourself that the basic scientists under whom you study are not "The Problem." They are merely introducing you to the inevitable contrasts within medicine itself between the values of basic science and those of healing. Fortunately, these contrasts enhance both fields: Medicine and science grow with each other in healthy (if occasionally stormy) symbiosis. And you and your classmates—thanks to your brushes with basic scientists—will think with a little more precision and a lot more fundamental understanding during that long stretch between your graduation from medical school and the end of your clinical lifetimes.

Exams

To be a physician is to be an exam taker. Medical school exams, national board exams, specialty exams, state licensing exams, recertification exams, and self-assessment exams—to name just a few—will be with you until you retire. Accepting this fact does not help much, though, when any particular exam comes up. The only consolation we can take, it would seem, is that our fellow examinees are probably feeling as miserable as we are. Studying with friends is probably the best prophylactic treatment for this stress. More about that later.

Too much sickness

Most people in our society are unaware of the rich variety of ways our bodies can be mis-assembled, broken, infected, worn out, or riddled with tumors. The occasionally grisly medical scenes most people witness on the media are soon mercifully forgotten. Not so for you. Your textbooks and clinical experiences will present you with an endless array of new human afflictions every day.

Most of us handle this stress with denial. "That looks awful. Good thing I'll never get it." Or, "Fortunately, I'm the wrong age, sex, race, occupation, religion to get hit with that one." And so we are usually not even consciously aware of this stress. Occasionally, though, when you are too tired, queasy, or otherwise physically down, you may feel it in any number of ways—from depression to "medical student's disease."

Rounds

The cornerstone of teaching in the clinical years of training, rounds, consists of a series of visits to the bedsides of patients. It is the process by which senior physicians look after the patients under their care. It also gives medical students and house officers in training an opportunity to see these physicians in action and thereby learn more about managing patients.

If that is all there is to it, why list it among the stresses of medical training? Based on what could whimsically be called the Socratic method, the conversation on rounds often consists largely of questions asked by the senior physician and answered by the trainees. However, if you cannot answer the questions completely, or, worse yet, you do not even know what the question is about, you can feel like a Christian in the arena conversing with the lions. The immediate impact of the experience is usually panic. The long-term impact (that is, after rounds are done for the day) is a serious and lingering doubt that one has chosen the right profession. "Will I ever know as much as the attending physician?" you ask. "No, never," comes a disquieting voice from some dark corner of your psyche.

Needless to say, such occasions, in which the risks of either humiliation or exaltation are so high, provide a rich medium for the proliferation of adaptive games known as "roundsmanship." For the senior physician there are "What am I thinking?" and "The latest article," among many. House officers and very bright students may also play the latter, but they must do so with very careful attention to casualness and humility. "Low profile" is an important game to master for those disquieting occasions when a question-you-cannot-answer has been raised and the senior physician is searching for someone to answer it. There are other games. Hundreds of them. You, yourself, will master many of them and probably invent a few of your own.

Call me "Doctor"

In our society we are all trained from birth to loathe the fraud and the pretender. Thereby we inevitably feel stressed by the title "Doctor" (or "Doctor-in-training") with which we are introduced—or, worse yet, are asked to introduce ourselves—to patients in the clinical years of medical school.

Participating in what feels like such a blatant masquerade usually stimulates any or all of a variety of feelings:

- *Hope* ("I sure hope they believe that story. Otherwise they'd never let me within ten feet of them.")
- *Self-loathing* ("How could such an otherwise honest person like me take part in such a sham?")
- *Fear* ("If they even suspected for an instant that I am a medical student, they'd throw me out so fast I wouldn't know what hit me.")

Take heart. Most patients in a teaching hospital already know they will be seen by medical students. Those that do not know that on admission will soon discover it from other patients, their doctor,

family, or hospital personnel. Moreover, your uniform often distinguishes you as a student. However, in the minds of many patients, there really is not any important difference between a medical student and a "real doctor." And, if you are in a caretaker role with a patient, they could not care less what you are as long as you are kind and competent—and you will be more competent than you think you are, having practiced your art on your fellow students before meeting your first patient. Finally, if it really bothers them or you (and it will not after a while), you can always "admit" to being a medical student. Do not be surprised if it does not make any difference to your patient.

Physical exams

Three values that you share with everyone entering medical school are
- "Respect other people's modesty,"
- "Do not touch strangers,"
- "Do not inflict physical discomfort on anyone."
Doing a rectal or pelvic exam, much less a thorough physical examination violates all three.

Take heart as you contemplate this fundamental stress-event:
- *All* of your classmates (not just you alone) will be experiencing anxiety with this.
- Before you get to your first patient, you will have practiced every part of the examination (except possibly pelvics, hernia, and rectal exams) on your classmates.
- Patients are generally no more uncomfortable with an examination by you than they would be with one by any physician.
- Your gentleness and reassurance have a powerful impact in minimizing the discomfort of your patients, even through uncomfortable procedures.
- With practice and experience, even you will become quite comfortable about doing physical exams.

Angry with patients

Most people going into medicine really do want to take care of people. That is why most of us are so astounded when we first find ourselves dangerously close to exploding at a patient. "How could a

kind, dedicated person like me be so angry at a helpless patient?" It is easy. Remember "patient" is just a role that everyone adopts—usually transiently—at some point or other in his or her life. "Good people" become "good patients" (that is, tolerant, cooperative, uncomplaining, appreciative). "Bad people" become "bad patients" (that is, demanding, uncooperative, endlessly complaining, unappreciative).

To make matters worse, even many "good people" behave in a way that many of us find particularly outrageous: They do not recover—or even improve, sometimes, despite our very best diagnostic and therapeutic work.

Special note: with the exception of patients with a few kinds of infections, most of your patients will not recover from their afflictions very fast. Of those who do, many will not return to the same state of health they enjoyed before you treated them. It is normal for physicians to feel frustrated and even angry about that sometimes.

When you feel this anger coming on, try not to let yourself fall into either of these traps:

- Complaining to the patient about it. (That just creates in patients a confused mixture of guilt, anger, and dependence that can impede future work with them.)

- Pretending to yourself that you are not really angry. This can lead to either or both of two bad outcomes: the development of any of the strain-reactions listed later in this report, and the high probability that your anger—having been officially declared non-existent—will come out later in dreadful ways of which you may not even be aware.

"Crocks"

Definition: A pejorative word for patients who refuse to get better despite your most impressive diagnostic and therapeutic efforts *or* patients who have physical complaints but no observable or measurable signs of pathology. It is not surprising that "crocks" tend to be roundly despised by young doctors: "crocks don't have anything 'interesting' "; "crocks are complainers"; "crocks just clog up beds and clinics where 'real patients' should be."

Warning: Look out when a patient gets labelled a "crock" because

- he or she may have a problem that medicine simply cannot yet document. The "crock" label has condemned many an innocent person to delayed medical care, and worse.
- Whether or not the "crock's" problem is "really medical," he has a real problem. His pain *is* painful. His itch *really* itches.

Odd finding: The use of the word "crock" varies inversely with the speaker's medical competence. That is because "crocks" are treatable, but often not by medication and operations, you have to investigate—gently—to find the emotional pressures that often contribute to "crockery." That takes good doctoring.

Final note: About half of the patients you treat, unless you go into pathology or anesthesiology, will have some degree of "crockery." Half. That means that the amount of satisfaction you will get from practicing medicine will depend a lot on how comfortable and competent you are with your "crocks."

Sexual stirrings

After working with patients and their bodies all day long, month after month, no patient is going to arouse you sexually, right? Wrong. You are not going to chat with your patients about how attractive they are, and you are certainly not going to act on your sexual feelings toward patients (That is even in the Hippocratic Oath), but chances are you will feel some sexual stirrings about a patient or two before your medical school days are over.

"Who, me?" I can hear you say, "Never!" "It's unprofessional, unethical!" Unfortunately, your own sexual machinery—the product of millions of years of successful reproduction—does not take ethics into account when it functions. It just functions.

To make matters worse, patients sometimes do or say things suggesting they think you are a very attractive or admirable person. This does nothing to quiet whatever stirrings you are feeling toward them at the moment. The enforced loneliness of medical school does not help the situation either.

Career versus home

Marriage (and also living together) in medical school can be supportive and can be tough. Many things are in short supply.

- *Limited money* may mean your surroundings will be modest, often frankly marginal. Moonlighting jobs will drain even more energy from you, and you may have to cope with all the stresses of a two-worker marriage.
- Medical training takes so much *energy* there often is not much left over for your spouse or lover, to say nothing of the children.
- Between class or clinical work, studying, nights "on call," and any jobs you may have, *time* can be critically hard to find for yourself.
- Even *emotional support* can seem to run low occasionally— especially on evenings when you come home exhausted from working and coping with the emotional needs of patients.

All of this was tough enough years ago when gender automatically decided who did what in the relationship: The woman always cooked and the man always took out the trash; the man's job determined geographic moves; the woman automatically took her husband's last name. Increasingly, few of these decisions are "automatic" anymore; instead, they demand understanding, patience, negotiation, and compromise.

Death and dying

Some of our patients will die. Even a good physician cannot prevent it. We all know it intellectually. But coming to grips with the reality of death—particularly the death of someone we are caring for— is always painful. The first time we "lose" a patient (notice the verb and the subtle implication that we have been careless or forgetful) is usually the hardest time.

It is hard for many reasons. We have come to know and value the patient, somewhat like a friend. And it is doubly hard if this patient reminds you of a friend or family member you particularly love. Usually he or she had come to trust you and sometimes think of you as "my doctor," even though he or she really knew you were "just" a medical student. "How could I 'let' this trusting friend die?" "Did I overlook something?" you may ask yourself. The death of a patient also underscores our feelings of helplessness and inadequacy as physicians. It can even make us feel guilty if we feel some secret relief at seeing our patient's suffering mercifully ended at last.

Before medical school, most of us had never seen anyone die, much less help someone who is making the awesome transition into death. Sometimes it reminds us of our own mortality, a grim prospect that physicians must work hard to dismiss from their minds. Finally, our first patient's death shatters one of our favorite myths: "If we just study enough and work hard enough, we physicians can 'save' everybody from death." It is a myth that dies hard.

4

Strain-reactions

Strain-reactions are just bad reactions to stress-events. They are usually bad because the stress has struck some aspect of our pre-set with uncanny and devastating accuracy. We each develop strain-reactions in our own particular way because our pre-sets are different. That is worth remembering, because you may sometimes feel not only defective, but also alienated if no one around you seems to be reacting the way you are. Do not panic. It is just your uniqueness showing.

Here are a few of the most common strain-reactions. You will probably recognize having had all of them at one time or another already in your life. You will have them often throughout your medical school years because medical school is rough, *not* because there is anything wrong with your mind.

Anxiety

This is the most common strain-reaction of all. It is common in medical training because it comes up when we fear we are about to do something wrong, when we have done something wrong, or when we are in the process of being told we did something wrong. All of this happens often in medical school.

We do not have to spend much time describing the more dramatic symptoms of anxiety—your muscles tighten, your heart pounds, you breathe hard, you get diarrhea, you have to urinate frequently, your mouth gets dry, and so on. All are part of your body's preparation for "fight or flight."

Anxiety has subtle forms, too, that you ought to know about: trouble getting to sleep, light-headedness, belching more than usual, abdominal bloating, tension headaches, irritability, trouble concentrating, overeating—to name just a few. We have listed these symptoms to help you recognize when you are *being* anxious but not necessarily *feeling* anxious. If you are experiencing these symptoms often, turn to "First-aid" in this book and take action.

Depression

This strain-reaction is as common as anxiety—a typical reaction to stress in medical school. The reason for this is that depression occurs "normally" under conditions that often prevail in medical school:

- You are furious with someone, but you cannot do anything about it. This is always happening—patients complain and refuse to improve, faculty and house officers are always creating more jobs for *you* to do, and almost no one is really pleased with your (considerable) efforts.

- You are not meeting performance expectations—yours and/ or someone else's. If you are perfectionistic—and you probably are or you would not have made it to medical school— this one is bound to cause trouble. Brace yourself: You will almost *never* meet your highest performance standards. There is just too much to do and learn.
- There is a gross imbalance in your life between what you are giving (working, studying, caring for others) and what you are getting back (love, admiration, approval, sex).

Like anxiety depression has symptoms that are subtle, as well as those that are obvious. *Obvious symptoms* include sadness, despair, self-doubt, low self-esteem, and occasional thoughts of suicide. *Subtle symptoms* include boredom, unusually pervasive fatigue, trouble concentrating, increased irritability, trouble getting to sleep or staying asleep, change in appetite (sex as well as food), constipation, vague abdominal pains, indigestion, and many more.

As with anxiety, you can *be* depressed without psychologically *feeling* depressed. If you are feeling unusual physical symptoms for which no physical cause can be found, consider the possibility that you might be depressed and take action. (See "First-aid.")

"Medical Student's Disease"

Everyone worries about his or her health occasionally. As medical students, interns, and residents, we probably worry about health more than most people our own age for four reasons:
- Our hours are longer and so we spend more time being tired.
- We are under more emotional pressure and so are more apt to develop the subtle physical signs of anxiety and depression.
- We each know thousands of dreadful diseases that begin with exactly the same kind of fatigue and other physical symptoms we are feeling.
- We are constantly working with patients whose conditions are constantly reminding us of how frail and mortal we are— reminders our non-medical friends are spared.

One of the worst things about this strain-reaction is that it somehow seems less honorable than the others. In fact, it would be almost comical if it were not so terrifying for its victims. "Fred's having

his annual case of Hodgkins again," or "Ann's SBE cleared dramatically after the exam last week."

Fears of having psychological disorders can also be a part of
"Medical Student's Disease." For example, schizophrenia is one of the
most commonly feared-but-absent disorders in this category. However
amusing these psychological forms of strain-reactions may be to
unsympathetic observers, they are deadly serious to their victims and
call for kind concern and prompt first-aid.

Having read all of this, be aware that being a medical student
does not magically protect you from real disease. Therefore, if you are
not feeling well, do not be too stoical about it. Check in with your
student health service.

Social strains

At times it is no fun living with someone who is in medical
school. You work and study peculiar hours, develop a variety of
psychological and physical strain-reactions, and are never well-rested.
Conversation definitely loses its sparkle. When you are tired, you are
dull (or even incoherent). When you are enthusiastic, it is all too often
about some medical topic that is either too technical or too graphic for
polite conversation. Despite the novels and movies that depict medical
professionals as sexually dashing and insatiable, the sex life of a
medical student may not live up to its glamorous billing. And finally,
there is the time problem. Even if you could remain emotionally
balanced, stay physically fit, make brilliant conversation, and maintain
creative sexual skills, you are simply not often away from work long
enough to be good company.

To make matters worse, when your families, friends, and lovers
finally allow themselves to feel angry about this, they often do not feel
comfortable talking about it. "I don't want to upset him/her. His/her
work is so important. With so many demands on him/her, it wouldn't
be fair for me to complain, too." And that can spoil the best of
relationships.

Depression is probably the most common reaction among the
people who love us. Sometimes they get around to being angry, but not
often enough. Occasionally things look perfectly peaceful until themes
of separation and divorce begin to appear in the conversation.

Fortunately, this particular strain-reaction, like all of the others, is potentially correctable if you discover it early. See "First aid."

Second thoughts

At some point in his or her career, almost everyone in medical school thinks one or several of the following thoughts: "What am I doing in this rat race?" "I am clearly not cut out for this business." "Why didn't I listen to my father's (wife's, husband's) advice and go into something reasonable like law (business, architecture, anthropology)?" "No one around me seems to have any of the same doubts about medicine that I do."

When you find yourself thinking one of these thoughts . . . and you probably will at some point . . . do not panic. Just remember that you are going through a private, lonely rite of passage that is shared by almost everyone in medicine.

5

First-aid

First aid is whatever you do to lessen the pain of a strain-reaction. First aid strategies can be divided into two groups:

- Good strategies—those that promote growth, strength, and competence, and
- Bad strategies—those that promote constriction, rigidity, and continuing tension for yourself and poor care for your patients.

Unfortunately (for the cause of growth), *both* kinds of strategies give immediate relief from psychological pain. As you might have guessed, though, our bias is to favor the good strategies over the bad ones. We have listed a few of each kind below, good ones first.

Good strategies

Talk about it. We listed this one first because it is the best one, as well as the simplest. Just find a reasonably sympathetic ear, for example:

Classmates with Whom You Feel Particularly Comfortable: People from the same ethnic or regional group might be the best choices, but any sympathetic classmate who feels some concern for you will suffice.

Ideally they might also ask a question or two that lets you understand even better how your particular strain-reaction felt. If they have not encountered that particular stress yet, it has the added advantage of helping them prepare for it in advance.

Classmates Who Just Went Through the Same Stress and Survived: Good for two reasons:

- Classmates do not need to hear all the details because they may have just had the same strain-reaction that you did . . . or at least one that is like it.
- They will usually welcome hearing your comments because it will open the door for them to talk it out with you, too.

A Sympathetic Loved One—Spouse, Lover, Family Member, Friend: Again, the benefit is not just yours, although it is a powerful antidote to your strain-reaction. It also lets the other person share more fully in your life, particularly if he or she does not have any other way of knowing how medical school is affecting you.

Informal Groups of Classmates—People with Whom You Eat, Take Coffee Breaks, Share a Cadaver, Complain, or Study: Comparing experience often provides you with not only more support, but also a variety of viewpoints about what the stress-event did to you and why.

Formal Groups of Classmates: In several medical schools, students have arranged to meet together regularly to exchange ideas and

feelings about what is happening to them. Although these groups may be leaderless, they usually work best with a trained leader.

Faculty: Although it does not work out well with all faculty, most want to know about any unnecessary or unusually heavy stresses their students are experiencing. Seek out especially those faculty members whom other students have found helpful.

Nurses and Aides: These can be your greatest allies, not to mention valuable resources. If treated warmly and respectfully, they can provide both the support and the practical advice you may need to get through many a strain-producing situation.

Walk away. Maybe this strategy should have been listed first because it is the first thing you can do to get relief quickly in a too-stressful situation. If your presence is not required (that is, for example, if you are not holding the surgical retractors), just leave the situation for a while—physically, by stepping out of the room, or psychologically, by staring at the wall. Then come back when you are ready. Nowhere is it written that you have to be present for every grim detail of a stress-event.

Follow up on your walk-away with a second first-aid strategy such as "Figure it out" so that the stress and your reaction to it can contribute to your continuing growth.

Sleep on it. Although not exactly a dynamic approach to problem-solving, giving yourself a full night's sleep (or as much of one as you can get) after a strain-reaction lets you gain more perspective (and hopefully more relief) before you start taking corrective action. It also gives you some physical recovery time. Our physical condition often makes the difference between mild annoyance and a full-blown strain-reaction in some stressful situations. Fatigue and viral infections (like flus and colds) are probably the most common culprits for making medical students vulnerable.

Figure it out. This consists of a very brief conversation with yourself that includes such questions as

- What stress-event caused my reaction?
- Was there more than one stress? What were they?
- What kind of strain-reaction did I have? What exactly did it feel like?
- How did my pre-set cause me to react to that particular stress?

A good idea is to combine several first-aid strategies—especially "Walk away" or "Sleep on it" followed by "Talk about it" or "Figure it out." By continuing to think and talk through the experience, you are continuing to learn and to grow.

Bad strategies

Ignore it. This is the worst of all bad strategies. It prevents you from learning enough about your own pre-set to give yourself warnings when you are about to suffer another similar stress-event. Finally, it may lead to your merely being *sensitized* to whatever stress-events you encounter rather than being *broadened* by them. Incidentally, it also prevents your loved ones from learning about you and your work.

Eventually, this kind of strategy can cause you unwittingly to seek professional roles that are more secure but less rewarding than others you might have enjoyed. It can also have the opposite effect—leading you to push yourself unknowingly into dangerously stressful roles merely because you need to maintain a sense of mastery under stress. Both outcomes can lead to major troubles when it is time to make your living in your chosen field.

Work it off. Channelling overwhelming emotional energy into work is a great way to complete work, whether it is studying medicine or caring for patients. Unfortunately, it does not lead to your learning much from a strain-reaction. Like "walk away," it is not bad first aid if you also take time to figure out the cause of your reaction. But it can lead to some bad professional choices later on in your career if it is the only first aid you allow yourself.

Self-medication. There are many medicating agents available in our society. Alcohol is the agent-of-choice in our profession. Marijuana and prescription drugs seem to be approaching similar prevalence, especially with medical students and house officers.

Although these and other drugs seem useful for numbing the pain of all kinds of strain-reactions, as well as for momentarily relieving boredom, they are really hazardous for physicians to rely on for two reasons:

- We tend to lead the kind of high-stress lives that frequently make self-medicating look attractive, especially the secret kind that helps us maintain the facade of the "strong, competent physician" while repairing inner shakiness, and
- We have the financial resources and access to drugs that make it easy to satisfy whatever longings for numbness we may have.

The best way to avoid alcoholism and other drug abuse is to become proficient at other first-aid strategies (q.v.), to cultivate your back-up supports (q.v.), and to build good preventive maintenance (q.v.) into your life style before you settle into your professional career. As we discover more about the enormity of the "impaired physician" problem, it is becoming clearer that this simple-sounding program is even more important than we ever thought.

6

Back-up Support

The best way to convert a stress-event into a growth-promoting experience is to talk with someone about it. This section focuses on cultivating the relationships within which these kinds of conversations can best be held.

Find a friend in your class

This is probably the most important thing you can do to ensure your survival in medical school. It is the key to the "talk about it" first-aid strategy, at the very least. It is also a key, under the pressures of medical school, to keeping your credentials as a humane human being. Sometimes it is not easy to find a friend with whom you are totally comfortable. If your feeling of being one of a minority is getting in the way, find somebody else in your minority. If there are not any, find someone who seems sympathetic.

Usually it is easy to find a friend. Classes, labs, and other study operations will throw you naturally into partnerships with various people, some of whom you will get to know well. Cultivate these relationships. When you are subdivided into small groups—for ex-

ample, for service on separate wards—be sure you have a local friend in those groups as well, if your usual friends are not included.

Some medical school classes have actually "formalized" the process of getting to know each other well. They meet several minutes before major lectures a few times a week so that class members can introduce themselves individually to the whole class by saying a little about their lives and interests. Formal "retreats"—usually with some faculty couples along—can accomplish the same purpose, if you have the facilities. Classmates who do not yet know each other well sometimes arrange to have meals or other social events together.

Establish a formal support group

This is optional, but it is a good thing to consider if you find yourself among several classmates having the same kind of strain-reactions under the same stresses. A faculty member or trained therapist can give the group more precision. In most medical schools, the psychiatry faculty or student health faculty can refer you to someone who is trained in working with such groups.

Nurses and aides

Nurses and aides can make your professional life inspiring or hellish, depending upon how they feel about you. But keeping a good relationship with them is as complicated as it is essential. For one thing, they will often know more about certain aspects of medical care than you will. Yet they have to react to you somewhat as though you were a card-carrying doctor. You both know you really are not.

There are no secrets to working out this complicated relationship. These tips may help:

- Be kind and respectful—even when you disagree.
- Whenever you find that you and they have different expectations of what each other is supposed to be doing together, accept the fact that you disagree, *clarify* together how and why you disagree, and *negotiate* an agreement you can both tolerate.

If you cannot reach an agreement, do it their way (if it does not jeopardize a patient's health or comfort), and then *talk it over* with a classmate before deciding whether or not to take the matter to a faculty member. Fortunately, such disagreements almost never arise in the first place, and you can anticipate generally friendly relationships with these co-workers.

Consider getting help

Somewhere in the course of medical school you may confront a situation that evokes a strong strain-reaction in you and that does not seem to bother your classmates much at all. *If it is a situation you are likely to encounter often in the course of your medical training and career,* think seriously about getting professional help for yourself.

To need help in this situation does not mean that you are defective or unusual. It means only that there is something in your background that predisposes you to have a strain-reaction in *particular kinds* of medical situations. In medical schools with good counselling services, up to 50 percent of all students use them at some time during their medical education. These services can take many forms—all the way from psychotherapy to instructive counselling on avoiding future stress by medically managing some situations more effectively.

The processes involved in counselling and psychotherapy are fairly simple—only three basically:

- Discovering issues that caused your strain-reaction,
- Learning how your early programming is no longer relevant *in its original form* to you in your struggle to become a mature, humane physician, and
- Using this new data about yourself to explore more effective, less wearing techniques for practicing medicine in the future.

Eliminating stress

We have described several coping strategies that involve releasing tension or getting reassurance. They are based on re-orienting yourself. However, there are things you can do to improve your medical training environment as well.

Fortunately, medical teachers and administrators can be roused to hear about problems and to correct alterable conditions that disturb medical students. Therefore, if there is something that really seems unreasonable—and you have established that classmates feel the same way—talk to the people in charge. If they cannot or will not help, move up the chain of command to departmental heads or deans.

Some problems are easily correctable, and some are not, but whoever is in charge of a program deserves to know if it is creating unnecessary stress for you and your classmates. Also, you deserve to have your requests heard and implemented if feasible.

Pick your mentor

Learning correct medical attitudes is as important as learning correct medical knowledge and medical skills. As humans, we learn attitudes from the people around us whom we admire. Not all of your teachers, sadly enough, will be people you fully admire. Some will be gruff with patients, some will be a little unclear in their logic, some will be autocratic with nurses and house officers, and some will seem personally idiosyncratic to you.

It is important, then, in each lecture series and on each clinical rotation, to identify the people you admire. If you cannot identify one particular faculty member you would like to use as a model, just borrow the admirable pieces of the ones who are available. If possible, select mentors whose backgrounds and experiences are similar to yours. It is easier to borrow style elements from someone who is like you. Introduce yourself to them, if it is convenient, so that they will know who you are. Faculty frequently do not *look* very receptive—usually because they are too busy to seem welcoming—but they usually *are* basically friendly. Watch them in action. Learn their "style" well enough so that you can "borrow" it when you need it in the future. Consider the ways in which your styles are complementary and those in which they are not. It is important to do this carefully, because it is the process by which you literally construct—piece by piece—the professional person you will become.

7

Preventive Maintenance

All of us can rise to an occasional challenge—cram for an exam, work through the night, stay with a dying patient. None of us can remain well-balanced, though, and keep practicing good medicine without periods of recovery. Because the study (and later the practice) of medicine consists of a series of strenuous challenges, the better you care for yourself, the better you will care for your patients.

This section is about "prophylactic life styles" . . . the art of minimizing stress and maximizing renewal. It is essential to performing well as a physician and, therefore, one of the important arts to be learned, practiced, and mastered in medical school.

Do not abandon your spouse

. . . or your friends or your lover or your family. Their love, interest, and concern for you is potentially the most powerful support in your life. Paradoxically, for medical students and physicians, there are more external obstacles to being good spouses, lovers, and friends, than for almost anyone else in our society. At first, usually, we have too little money. Always, we have too little time, energy, and emotional zest because of the demands of our work. Consequently, we have to be more careful than most people that our careers do not seduce us away from the people we love.

This requires careful, disciplined planning: not letting your office hours gradually build up too far as your practice gets busier, arranging to have colleagues cover your practice so that you and your family can get away undisturbed, budgeting significant amounts of money and time for recreation and vacations.

Sounds simple. Actually, by the time you finish medical training, this could be very hard indeed. You will have to unlearn much of what medical training encourages you to do—postpone gratification, sacrifice your own (and often your loved ones') convenience and comfort for the sake of your patients, and put what little money you have into your career. In short, you will be conditioned to making medicine your first priority. Remember that this is an almost-universal hazard in the lives of physicians and of those in medical training.

Play and have fun

About the last thing on your mind as you enter medical school is playing and having fun. "The harder you work," the saying goes, "the better you will do in medicine." Not quite. All work and no play will

merely exhaust and diminish you. Cultivating the ability to play or otherwise disengage from your work is one of the most important *disciplines* to cultivate in medical school. Whether it is athletic or aesthetic, stimulating or soothing, plan for at least one mini-event each day and something special each week. Consider it a vital part of your medical work. Also be aware that the values subtly (and sometimes unintentionally) underlying your medical training will fight constantly against it. "Keep working," goes the message, "and don't squander your time, energy, and money on anything frivolous."

It is a matter of balance. "Mid-career burn-out" and many of the "impaired physician" phenomena are often the tragic outcome of years of emotional neglect—ignoring or postponing too long meeting needs that exist outside of work.

Practice what you do best

The life of a physician can be lived in dozens of ways. Clinicians, administrators, teachers, and researchers in medicine can have life styles that are entirely different from each other. Even the professional lives of full-time clinicians can vary dramatically if they practice different specialties.

After you have taken a good look at what different kinds of physicians do for a living, and at the personalities of the people who inhabit each professional niche, choose a career that fits your personality. If you are drawn to taking bold, decisive action, consider careers in such fields as surgery or emergency-room medicine. If you prefer deliberate, contemplative work, investigate specialties like internal medicine or psychiatry.

Why is making the right career choice so important? Because if you choose a career that does not fit your personal style, you will spend your professional life fighting your work. If you make a good career choice, you will enjoy your work and really look forward to beginning each day.

One final word: Your family may have some definite ideas about career choices for you—surgery because it is dashing, or research because it is noble. Take them with a grain of salt. You, not they, will be the one to live your professional life.

8

Final Thoughts

Because we have been focusing on the stresses, strains, and dangers of medical training, we have not said much about what a good choice you have made in deciding to become a physician. The rewards in medicine from helping people, from having intellectual stimulation, and from enjoying reasonably comfortable surroundings are great. We tend to feel more satisfied and less regretful about our career choices than any other profession. And we have more opportunities to see directly the beneficial impact of the work we labor so hard to perfect.

Good luck!